The Anthology of Cashmere Thoughts
Volume 2

By: Mr. Talik Jordan

To my Mother,

Thank you for being you and raising me the way you did. Nothing but a fantastic job. Forever my G.O.A.T

Dedication:

I dedicate this to myself because I am surprised once again. Being the author of one book is cool, but two made me want to give myself a standing ovation. I have created and distributed a product that will forever be a part of history. Shoutout to myself. I also must acknowledge those who believed and encouraged me to continue even when the vision was unclear. If you are reading this right now, I greatly appreciate you, and congratulations on being a part of Imperfect Legacy.

The Preface to my Cashmere Thoughts Vol.2:

When I first created "The Anthology of Cashmere Thoughts," I knew it would be the only book I would make. Honestly, I was surprised that I even started a book; it never seemed like something I would ever be into doing. Twenty percent of that thought was thinking I did not have the capabilities to create something like that, and the other eighty percent was that I DID NOT KNOW WHAT TO TALK ABOUT. Write a book about my life; it seems unreasonable because I am just starting it. Talk about experiences from my upbringing and college; I have had some experiences that are movie worthy, but I do not want too much information about myself being out there. However, it is wild to see my poems are public because some speak of vulnerable moments that were a part of my life at a specific time. Eventually, I became comfortable with writing because this became a way of venting out emotions I did not feel like speaking on. Here we are with volume two of Cashmere Thoughts; I feel more energetic with this one. I wanted to approach this book differently from the first volume. In my eyes, volume one was a success because I did not expect to receive the number of books purchased (To the ones who bought it, you already know how I feel. From the bottom of my heart, I genuinely appreciate you because you gave me the motivation to create more poems and another Cashmere Thoughts.). With volume two, I wanted to put some poetry in it but also explain them thoroughly, potentially leaving you with some food for thought. That food for thought could get you thinking about life or hopefully motivate you to do specific things to help you obtain a goal. After the first one, I felt that I was slighting the individuals reading the book because of this beautiful thing called "perspective". I do not want to leave them with any conception of confusion while reading the poems. There will be an area called "Point of Emphasis" after each poem that will explain the reason for the abovementioned poem. So, with that being said, I hope you enjoy this version of the book series you've started to love called Cashmere Thoughts!

4

Poems

Cardinal Sin
Moment of Time
Computer LUV
For 1 Night
Back 'N Forth
I'm Just Tired
Fearful Success
Spiritual Richness
Why isn't There a Class on Patience?
On Sight
Excuse-Moi (Excuse Me)
The Getaway
A Dedication
All on You
Jollity
As a Man
As a Woman
Forgiveness

Wise words from Kendall B. about The Anthology of Cashmere Thoughts Vol. 1:

"This collection of poems, "The Anthology of Cashmere Thoughts", really encapsulates what it means and how it feels to be a young adult in this society. With every read, I felt this book was just a testament to how none of us are alone in our journey through life. A stunning collection that I will revisit for years to come".

Wise words from Coleman S. about The Anthology of Cashmere Thoughts Vol. 1:

"The courage of putting your thoughts on paper and to publishing it, despite the thoughts of others is very inspiring. Especially those from your specific background. Reading the different poems felt as if I was a part of the author's mind to the point where I could relate. Specifically, the poem titled "20's", going through the mental change of your 20s, you hear a lot of things that are supposed to be said. The poem was real, ups and downs with the emotions of your 20s, the perspective of your 20s, and trying to maintain your 20s to just name a few. It put me in a space where I understood that I can control my 20s, my perspective, and ups and downs. Words are just words, but the people behind them give them life. Understanding the author was raw and emotional made it okay for myself to feel in general. I really appreciate not on that poem but every poem that the author pours into. It made it genuine, and we need those people in society. I give the Cashmere Thoughts series a 10/10. It's more than just words, it's passion and love. Cannot wait until the next one drop!"

· Welcome to a Space ·

· Where Cashmere Thoughts are Placed ·

Cardinal Sin

A wise man once said,
"Why everything that's supposed to be bad, makes me feel so good?"
Every time I see you, I fantasize about things I shouldn't
You whisper innocently, "You envision the same"
Our moral compass
Conflicted with which direction
Could bring pleasure w/o pain
You're bound by a social contract
You fear to break
I'm bound by statements to a lover whom I tell, "I'll always stay"
My words used like a double edge knife
Because I mumbled them while
Envisioning I'm speaking to you each night
Risks are meant to be taken
Hearts can endure breaking
The life we want is beyond the thought of debating
Being analytical is what got us far in life
But for this moment, emotions over logic are the only thing that
sounds right.
In this seductive world
You're what a man dream of
The right amount of temptation
Plus pleasure that's dangerous to feign for
And if I take this vow
To break this code of conduct
I insist it is with
The woman I plan to spend
More than eternal life with
Even in moments of distress
Us being connected would be bliss
Take this as a consolation of my inclination toward you
Because inevitably we'll have our moment of truth

Point of Emphasis for Cardinal Sin:

Beginning this poem with a lyric from the song Addiction by YE (Formerly known as Kanye West), I heard this verse and instantly resonated with it. If there was only one question to ask our creator, the best one would have to be that question. Temptation, lust, and enticement are many words that could describe a feeling that every human on earth internally adores. How do these emotions enter our bodies? What chemical reaction goes off in our brains to have us feigning that temptation? Of course, dopamine has something to do with it because we disguise this "pleasure" as a reward, and because our bodies live off habits, it considers temptation a part of our daily regime. But what happens when that temptation is for another human? Especially one that is considered off-limits. It is unbelievable how society has these unwritten rules about who a person can date and not date. Your friend messaged someone on social media you found attractive a couple of months ago, and now it's like if you tried to talk to that person, it appears either weird or surreptitious-like behavior. Someone you know dated another attractive person, and they broke up. You could have the opportunity to get to know them and build something great potentially, but morally, it would be deemed wrong. I agree with these rules eighty-five percent of the time because 1.) I do not want to be intimate with another woman that was also intimate with someone I know of, and 2.) There are too many women to go after the same one somebody has already dealt with. But as I have gotten older and received more life experiences, that 15% tends to pop up and suggest that we even go higher in some circumstances. Even though I say these things, it is hard to proceed with the action. Honestly, I would not look at myself the same in the mirror performing these types of activities. But, on the same spectrum, a small thought in my mind whispers, "Forget about what everyone thinks and do what makes you happy at the moment because that is all that matters." People are doing what makes them happy; why can't you receive that same enjoyment? Truthfully, I wrote this poem about a specific person and was going back and forth on whether I should state this in the book. I was worried about people's perspective of me and did not want to be considered a "sleazeball", but there I go caring about what people think again. It is a thought, not an action; how many intrusive thoughts go through your mind daily? No man can say I badmouth them towards a woman; I wish I could say no one did the same for me. Going back to the mysterious lady, even if the opportunity prevailed, I still would not take it seriously, but the thought of it would be excellent. I know this doesn't sound good, but other people also have these thoughts about individuals that are part of their friend group or met because of a friend. I want you to realize that it is okay to have unconventional thoughts; you are human and it's part of our nature. However, do not have sly-like behavior such as plotting on your friend to mess up so you can steal his woman or as a woman, creating a false narrative to your friend to make her break up with her boyfriend so you can get with him. Respect is still significant in this situation, and if you can keep a solid barrier to it, things will be okay.

Moment of Time

For this moment in time
Let's push respect to the side
For this moment in time
Let's make our concealed emotions arise
Your seductive resting face
Has me stuck in a bind
& I'll be lying if I said I didn't want you
For more than one time
It's funny to know
You don't realize this
Some thoughts need to stay thoughts
But for you,
I'm willing to take the risk
You're too dangerous because you have me testing my morals
Got me asking myself,
"Are the ones you say you close with
Really here for you?"
But that's the lusting mind in control once again
We need to just remain cordial
But,
If I was a betting man
I'll put it all on the fact that you
Feeling the same
& for me to find out just takes
Searching up your name
Thinking about what I'm going to say
Your photos are enticing me
But as soon I'm about to send a message
I realize this isn't the right thing
You were the lover to a mutual
So I can't go against the code
But,
I swear I'm at the point where I'm about to fold
But I can't fold under pressure
Even though this moment is fighting with all it's might
I feel this battle would end in TKO with one messaging the other one night
There's a lot of secrets that's never been told in this world
Let's add on to that list & pursue the moment of temporary love

Point of Emphasis for Moment of Time:

Like the poem Cardinal Sin, it follows the concept of the unwritten rule once again. Close to 8 billion people in this world, and in your lifetime, how many people do you think you'll see? Consider the people you have met from middle school, high school, and some college. Some can say about a couple of thousand, and for others, lower than that. Out of that number, how many of them had a lasting effect that even to this day you stay in contact with them? If you were to take the ratio of how many you currently keep in touch with to how many you have met, that number would likely be low. My point is that some people never make it out of their hometown or state to venture and find new people to connect with, and what ends up happening is you are stuck with the same dating pool that your friends are connected to as well. Next, I must ask the burning question, why does it matter? Why does it matter who your ex-girlfriend/boyfriend is dealing with if you moved on and are "happy"? Why does it matter if your friend is entertaining someone you used to entertain a few years ago? Does it have something to do with being egoistic? Does it have something to do with being greedy? This unwritten rule has killed so many "what if" moments that it's preposterous. I understand the notion of "if it's meant, it'll be," but I look at this situation the same way I look at the lottery. If you do not play any numbers, there is 0 chance of you being able to profit from the winnings. It would be best if you entertained the idea of getting to know someone to know how well it would work for you. I must play devil's advocate in this situation because it has been happening for years but seems so prevalent now. I like to look at situations like this as a battle of consideration vs. contentment. As you age, contentment will start to show its importance in everyone's life. The more you branch out, the more you realize how unconventional people are. Some extroverted people do not mind venturing into things that are out of the norm, but the rest of us, do not care to partake in any of those things. If it walks like a duck and quacks like a duck, it better be a duck and not some other mythical creature. After stating everything above, does it matter what someone does with their life if they are not causing harm and are happy? Please think about that question and analyze it with areas in your life, and you will see how much caring you put into situations that do not have a detrimental effect on your life.

14

Computer LUV

Living in a world where I can see what's on your mind 24/7
Analyzing your photos has me realizing I have to say this confession
I need to get to know you
Even if it's for a split second
One laugh is all that's needed
To make a good impression
Out of all the messages in your notifications
Mine was the lucky one to get picked
The exchange of words I use
Has you realizing I could be legit
Now I've entered the qualification phase
First is to send a picture to the group chat to see if they know anything
Nothing comes back around so I pass with an A
Next is to go to the photos to see if anyone commented anything
You didn't like what you seen but,
It's still decent enough to get a B
Last is to look through the friends list to see if I know who knows you
A good amount, but you find me attractive so you can let that slide too
This is the new world that's in the palm of our hands
Which could be a blessing & a curse
If one truly understands
Miscommunication & bold accusations
Are what's fueling some hiding behind these electronic pages
But glad you see I'm different
without having me saying it
And though my words are powerful
The actions behind it are more impactful
Leaving you intrigued & questioning if it's too good to believe
But this isn't a facade
More so a fantasy of your dreams
I'm more than a charming prince coming to save your life
I'm committed to the position of being your husband, would you care to be my wife?
A bit fast but why waste time when you know what you like,
What you love,
What you admire,
&
What you adore,
I'm just tired of

Placing a key in an unhinged door
So I'll leave you with another message to show that it's real
Hopefully this computer will direct me to a love that's everlasting & real

Point of Emphasis for Computer LUV:

I cannot start this without giving a special shoutout to Zapp Band and Shirley Murdock for writing the legendary song Computer Love. This poem provides a snapshot of what it is like dating in current times. Like everything in this world, there are pros and cons to getting to know someone; at times, it can become overwhelming. A percentage of the world is still traditional with the method of introducing themselves whenever they see someone in public. Positive outcomes still can come out of this method, but it may sometimes feel that approaching someone through social media first is the better option. Your social media pages can be resumes showing your physical attraction and intellect. Though it could be skewed, this is a way for an individual to comfortably analyze you and conclude if they are interested in what they see. Something simple as receiving a like on your pictures or a direct message indicates that this person is interested in you. In-person, those body language signs can also be skewed, and for some individuals, they are automatically closed off to anyone that approaches them due to previous experiences. Another reason social media is the better option is because it is more of a safer approach. I had heard multiple stories from women that stated how they were forced to give their number to an individual because of the actions some women faced when they did not give out their number. Some bad apples spoiled the pack, meaning some uninteresting individuals made it slightly tricky for genuine individuals with the potential to get to know someone. On the contrary, when you have "it" like that, these issues are not a problem majority of the time. Individually, you would have to do an internal audit on whether you can approach in person or if your social media presence is more robust and reliable.

For 1 Night

Temporary Love feels so enticing when it comes to you
The euphoric rush we have will become addicting soon
And even though we just met on the dance floor,
It seems like you're the one I've been SEARCHIN for
I have the problem of moving TOO FAST
Creating all these promises
Promising to HEAL YOUR HEART when truth be told
I don't even want to start
I just want to enjoy the time I have with you now
Drinking this reposado while finding a song with the beat tempo slowed down
Living like a ROLLING STONE because I'm always on the go
May need REHAB but I'll relapse soon as I touch back on the road
That's why being with me for ONE NIGHT ONLY is the best way to go
No need to get attached to a broken soul
It's 3am
And your temptations invade your thoughts
With your actions slowly caving at the same time
INVITE ME to your home
Is what's repeating in your mind
Even though it's CLOUDED
It still knows what it wants on the inside
From our conversations
We're both missing out on intimate affection
Reasons to believe us being in the same vicinity was destined
No WASTED TIME will be allowed
No BLUFFIN will be announced
We both have intentions of showing the other person how they been MISSIN OUT
Silent agreements of keeping it cordial after this is said and done
But we'll agree to any terms of conditions as the night intensify for us
We've BEEN AWAY from the reality of life for a while
So this moment was well needed thus,
Leading to wonder what's next to discuss
As we leave the resort
A kiss goodbye is given to have us remember the night and build up the temptation for the next time
As I look through my messages I see you saved your name as ALL MINE

This how I know we mesh because I made that my name too for whenever I hit your line
"LOST KIDZ GET MONEY", is the motto we live by
Glad to see I finally met someone on my same type of time

Point of Emphasis for 1 Night Only:

The discography of Brent Faiyaz inspired this poem. Even today, when I listen to One Night Only, it gives me frissons like it was my first time hearing it. Also, the Wasteland LP was remarkable, from the cinematic production of it to the storytelling, simply ten out of ten. Temporary Love was the main idea tossed around in this poem. Is it wrong to be a temporary lover when you have no other responsibilities or obligations? Is it possible to believe that an individual could be more fitting to be only a temporary lover? I ask these questions because being promiscuous is a thing in this world. Though some cultures/religions shun this action, it still does not answer whether it is wrong to classify with that term, especially when you are being safe with your methods. For example, if a man was raised in a polygamist upbringing but was pressured to change because of Western traditions, is he inappropriate for reverting to what he believes in/was raised on? Of course, most of us in the United States will say HE IS 100% wrong, but this place we live on is called Earth, not the United States of Earth. It would be best not to shun things foreign to you because you are ignorant of the subject. I was not raised to be a polygamist or anything, but I do not disgrace those who believe in it either. Switching gears, I wanted to focus on how amazing it is to find someone with the same beliefs as you regarding specific situations. Take the poem, for example; the two individuals are both comfortable with everything and end up having a great time with the intention of meeting again. Furthermore, I want to understand why being honest in this society is so hard. If you only want a short-term investment with an individual, why do you not state that in the beginning, so time is well-spent? This question is posed for both genders because it seems like a flux of people saying one thing and doing the opposite. You only can know what a person may be interested in once you ask them; there is no need to lie.

Back 'N Forth

It's me, then it's you
It's you, then it's me
Maybe more me than you, but that is hard to believe
At times this feels like an interesting generation to date
But the same can go with any other timeframe
We admire the older ones for the security of love they have
And at times,
They admire the freedom and accessibility that's in our grasp
Hard to detect what's deemed the best
Because comparing could lead you down a road of distress
We're all just individuals longing to be loved
Yearning to be connected with someone that goes beyond the above
But because of the power this one emotion has
We water down the true feelings we tend to have
The reasons are endless
Hurt, guilt, shame, and most of the time afraid
99% of the time afraid because neither one of us wants to feel played
A cold heart brings a cold life
And living amongst this hypothermic shocked world,
The true battle is
Differentiating which emotion is wrong or right
Which side are you fighting for?
Cave into societal norms
Or go against the grain of what you believe more?

Point of Emphasis for Back 'N Forth:

If someone wanted a screenshot of how it is trying to date in current times, this would give the perfect image. When did we go wrong, or have we always been wrong? One of my favorite parts of this poem is when I commented on generational differences. I cannot count how many times I've talked to older gentlemen who state how they would have been if they had had Instagram, Twitter, and Snapchat during their upbringing, and I truthfully understand. Those social media channels can bring many positives into an individual's life, but there are times I would trade it for what they had back in their times. Accessibility is a significant feature that goes a long way because back in those times if you did not approach a person and get their contact information, it's a high chance you would never see them again. Vice Versa, if that happens nowadays, you are bound to know someone who knows someone who knows who you are looking for. From my perspective, the connection was more genuine back then than it is now because, honestly speaking, it is dangerous out here. I know the "trust issues" statement has become over-saturated, but it is true because the things both genders are doing out here are wild to believe. Then you also must throw in the concept of not knowing an individual's true intentions; many of these things are an issue in any generation, but the abovementioned things are more prevalent now. Another thing that has poisoned my generation is the battle of being cold-hearted. How many times can I get over on a person? How can I express my emotions without looking too sensitive? At a younger age, this was my mindset at times, and I thought this was the best way to maneuver within society, but I learned the hard way that this was not the best option. Many people blame the music for insinuating this mindset to the masses, which I slightly agree with, but simultaneously, it does take the individual to decipher entertainment from reality. Everyone tries to avoid being hurt; truthfully, you will get hurt multiple times. Hurt will not go away, so building a lair to protect your heart is okay for a period, but if you do not want to be lonely and without genuine love for the rest of your life, you will have to go out and take a chance to find happiness. Looking back at the situations I encountered, I was the problem most of the time because I was scared to trust the woman I was involved with. I didn't trust them because I was afraid to give my heart to someone just for them to play around with it. I now realize that this method could be successful in the short-term but can have severe long-term damage if not learned how to shut it off.

I'm Just Tired

I'm so tired of writing about this emotion
Feels like I'm playing a non-stop record titled,
"Commotion"
How does it go away?
Tried telling myself not to think about it
Like my brain is going to obey
Switch your mindset up
Because "negative thoughts are like a leech"
Telling myself to do that is like
Telling a devoted preacher not to preach
It's a part of me
It's a part of my routine
Even when I do not want it to be
I thought I fought this feeling off
But I see myself slipping again
Don't want to vent no more
Tired of hearing myself sound like this
Letting out a silent cry and no one
Senses these tears of emotion
The invisible enemy is at it again
Why do I conform to who the enemy
Says I am
I'm so conflicted, I just don't understand
I feel so lost in myself
While trying to figure out who I am
And I do not know who that is anymore
It's like I psych myself up with all these things
Just to give up before success is through the door
But is it giving up when it feels like this is not your calling?
Is it giving up by changing your life before you end up falling?
Not being able to get back up
Eyes blinded by your failures now
It's just all overwhelming, and I do not know how to fix it now
I even got to the point where I was ashamed to speak to God
Because it feels like disappointment is the only thing leaving my mouth
I see the spiritual signs, but the physical ones say different
Hard to keep my faith when my physical is tripping
I've been in developing times before, so I can manage to get out
But how long will it take till I can dig myself out

Point of Emphasis for I'm Just Tired:

Poetry like "I'm Just Tired" reflects on developing times in my life but can also be relatable to another person. I write things like this to help those needing assistance expressing these emotions. Some feel they cannot because no one will listen or understand where they are coming from. I am no therapist, but I know a few things from experience. When a moment becomes overwhelming, you must step back and realize how much of a small period it is in your lifetime. My old supervisor used to have a bunch of tally marks written on the board, and each day he would look at the board before starting his day at work. I remember asking what that is supposed to symbolize, and he said each tally mark represents a year in a 75-year-old person's life. He was in his mid-thirties, so half of his tally marks were already crossed out. That stuck with me to this day because when we think about these ages that are far away, we do not visually understand how close it is. What got me was seeing how 75 tally marks did not cover half of the board and visually how it looked when 35 of those marks were crossed out. Whenever you get a chance, I want you to do the same thing: create 75 tally marks, cross out the amount comparable to your age, and look at how many you have left. After analyzing, consider if you are satisfied with what you have completed and if there is more you could do. Whatever your idea of success and happiness is cannot be judged because it is all about what brings joy into your life. If not, that is okay because there is still time to make substantial changes regardless of the amount available. Look up the successful people in the world and see when they first reached a level of success. That type of realization could be frightening for some, but it is something that needs to be done instead of realizing it when it is too late. To my people who have inner battles every day of the hour, the pendulum eventually swings back to its opposite side. Do not let this minuscule moment have a longing effect on your life. Lastly, the main trait that stops a person's success is not being pessimistic or procrastination; it is ignorance. People love the saying, "Ignorance is Bliss," but the older I become, the more I realize how much I hate that phrase. This statement does not go well in any category from personal, business, or financial; being unaware in any situation can jeopardize whatever you have going on. So why is it such a famous statement? It pushes the notion that it is okay to take the easy route and conform to what is happening at the time. Historical events show why we should not conform to certain things, but people still do. Those are the same people who unintentionally stop other people from growing in different aspects because they are only used to things being one way. You must realize who these people are in your life and disassociate from them when it comes to specific topics regarding your life. Learning that is the hardest thing to do because we are human and like being around people we are comfortable with. However, there comes a time when you have to grow up and make decisions that can better your life first. Be comfortable in ignorance or make a life knowledgeable in all subjects; the choice is yours.

Fearful Success

Congratulations on your accomplishments
Congratulations on overcoming harsh comments
Congratulations on beating statistics
& congratulations on becoming unforgiven
To yourself that is
Surrounded by four walls
In your lonesome
Is a battle even the strong find tough to win
As I scroll down my call log
Who is worthy enough to hear my pain
My cry for help that's overshadowed by the joy I bring
Crazy to see two people here for the same thing
Different emotions on both sides
But one cannot explain
Is it just me?
Or is it not?
I look in the mirror for a definitive answer
But my eyes have a hard time adjusting to this close shot
I go back to my bed and stare into the dark
Feeling so much peace at this time
But as I really begin to get comfortable,
Why are negative statements screaming in my mind?
I go back to the mirror to see if someone is in there with me
But all I see is my internal enemy
The one that puts a timer on every objective in my life
The one that tells me nothing I do will ever be right
The one that tells me the love I receive is all lies
I can go on for hours, but if I do
I'll start to believe the things it tells my mind
What you think is what you become
And that is what scares me the most
& I don't have time to vent to someone
Because they have their own problems they host
Everything is a perspective
So how do you know what's right & wrong
As much as these negative thoughts consume me
They also fuel me to keep on
What's scary the most about this
Is the answer will not come until the outcome is done

I'm gifted with the curse of wanting to succeed in life
& honestly, I wouldn't want it no other way
I'm addicted to this pain & rehab can't take it away
Nor will I let it
Just let me be
Drowning in my success & pain
Is a content decision for me
Is this wrong to ask?
Is this wrong to think?
The person I look for an answer from
Is the one whose reflection is staring right back at me
Of course it's going to agree
Telling me everything I want to hear
But as soon as silence comes back around
It goes against me
Like it doesn't know who I am
Stressful conversations are all that come from this bind
That's why writing out my thoughts is me rebelling against my mind
The Battle of Me seems like it will forever go on
With no white flag in sight
But I promise not to let it
Deter it from my purpose in life

Point of Emphasis for Fearful Success:

How long will it take to be successful? A vague question that has a vague answer that comes with it. Though success is subjective, a particular type can hold so much power in our minds. This power can be in the form of an influx of materialist things to your freedom. What do you want from your life, and why do you want these things? Simple questions could have intricate answers because your version of success will differ the higher your class status. The ultimate success is the freedom to do whatever I enjoy with my life. That does not include a set number in my bank account, travel vacations, or luxury materials. It is just the mindset of not having to worry about the price of an item, the time I have available to do something, or questioning whether I can help someone without hurting myself financially. On the other spectrum of this poem is the battle with self-doubt. How does the origin of self-doubt come into an individual's life? Is it only a form of comments about you, things you feel you are not good at, or is it both? As you read this, these are the questions you must consider to gauge how severe your self-doubt is and how your doubt developed.

Spiritual Richness

What you believe is what you achieve so they say
I want the house on the hill with a private lake
I meant I have the house on the hill with a private lake
Notifications with my tail number
Are what gets me excited for the day
Being greeted as soon as I walk through the threshold,
"Good evening Mr. Jordan", while handing me
My Michelin star plate
Exquisite wines, exclusive dining
Don't have to own a Piguet to know
Everything is coming to me in perfect timing
But everything was already perfect before the tangible things had arrived
I was rich in the spirit that's how it gravitated toward my mind
I felt the glory, I felt the pleasure way before I had the butterfly door Tesla
Way before I could take a trip because I wanted a change in the weather
I drop a tear in my S-Class whenever I think about my past
Would wipe them away with my Hundreds
But this AMEX that's the color of my skin
Is the only thing I have
They used to scream out negro and now I see why
Because the power this Black Man has could make Warren Buffet cry
I'm happy that I have and I'm happy to spar
It's so much money out here, you just have to find a way to make your share.
Teaching me the game is all I ever need, I already had the hustle and the drive
I just needed to believe
I like to think these traits are what got me here
This place of Zen that tend to go unaware
Peace to the mind and peace to the soul
Obtaining this aura will bring success tenfold
They don't tell you to know yourself for no reason
The powers you could possession are inevitable
Like the upcoming seasons
However,
After obtaining these things I still felt I had no meaning
What was I lacking or truly not seeing?
It was a good community, love, and genuine happiness
Having tangible things only brought temporary attraction

Attraction that I felt would always be infinite
Infinite because of all the hard work I did to get it
To get it took a crazy amount of sacrifice
So much sacrifice that even to this day I'm paying the price
The price of losing long term connections with the ones I love
But tell me is it really love if they left even after I explained the things above?
It's okay though because this is part of the journey
The journey to elation with no negative thoughts returning
Find your peace of mind because it's all we have
"What you put in, is what you get out",
The mantra you have to remember to grasp

Point of Emphasis for Spiritual Richness:

Money is power and power is freedom. Freedom is the main thing you realize that you will need. I like to believe that being successful comes with understanding the traits an individual has to possess. How do you know which ones are required? After studying different successful people, I realized they didn't have something unobtainable to grasp; they all had patience. The trait of being patient is so valuable but hard to contain for some people, including myself. I do not know where this lack of patience comes from, but I continuously improve on removing it from my life. I will say having patience is included in multiple ways because I can see how I am patient when dealing with someone who has their emotions unstable, but when it comes to investing in a skill or financial ideas, I want things to happen right at that moment. It's the same trait and requires the same type of skills, so what makes it challenging to manage when it comes to certain things? I wish I knew the answer to this question when I was younger because I realize it came from being ignorant of the situation. Ignorance being a blissful thing is horrible because of the lack of knowledge it can bring in the future. However, this is what growth, manifestation, and teaching are put onto this Earth for. It is incredible to be brought up in a generation where I can know the answers to anything I want to know, and it will also show a step-by-step guide of how to gain or complete something. Spiritual Richness is available for every person and can be very subjective because it is all about what that person considers richness. Some believe it's the accessibility to do and buy what you want, while others believe it is about having things that cannot be bought. I like to think that it is both! I need both because I cannot lie; traveling is a fantastic thing everyone should do, but I also understand how being able to share these wonders with people you care for are very important as well. Everything on this Earth needs balance and understanding areas that need improvement in your life will be something you are continuously working on. In the meantime, write down a list of things you feel you need to improve on and then list things you think you are handling well. For example, I lack balance in my life and excessive spending, but I have the patience and determination to complete any task. You'll realize the great things about yourself, areas that need improvement, and why you need to improve it.

Why isn't there a class on patience?

Live fast, die young
Is the motto some live by
Making it to the age of 30…
Might as well say our social security check is near by
Who came up with the idea that faster was better for everything?
In some cases it may be
But not for everything
I think about my life plans I had mapped out for when I turned twenty-five
Now past that age, I start thinking I must've been out of my mind
Married with a family
3 kids to be exact
& That's hilarious because nowadays I cringe at the price of Similac
Plus I do not want a relationship,
I'm still figuring myself out
Figuring out if I want to go to the club
Or take someone special out
Why isn't there a class on patience?
In a world that's telling me to move fast
Obtaining all of these things, so these companies can compare and contrast
On whom they feel is the best for their company
They're going to pick the less fortunate because they can manipulate them with less money
Why isn't there a class on patience?
Teaching me to be mindful of who I share my energy with
So many lost souls I'm attached to because I wanted it quick
Didn't understand the long-term effecting contract I signed
When our bodies connected
Now I feel what you feel
Can't believe I'm so emphatic
Why isn't there a class on patience?
To let me know everything is going to be fine
Some rely on the good book and others, it's the spiritual signs
Waiting on confirmation that our little life will show its purpose in due time
Why isn't there a class on patience?
I wish there was a class for patience
Because patience is the key to surviving here and any other nation
I mean look at our predecessors and all the things they were facing
With our current resources and their patience,

———

29

We would be unstoppable,
Controlling our country's population
And that's the reason why
They want all of us to stay complacent
It makes sense now
Why they're never teaching a class on patience

Point of Emphasis for Why Isn't There a Class on Patience?:

"Making it to the age of 30 might as well say our social security check is nearby" is a memorable line whenever I read this poem. It is unbelievable how a specific age could seem so far from you until you are that age. Like many people in my age range, thirty sounds like an age known for establishment. Whenever I thought of thirty, I felt that all problems would go away (hypothetically speaking), and I would be stepping into a new chapter of my life. In some cases, that may be true, but for others, that thought is just used as a mental getaway from all the stress one may be dealing with currently. This mindset leads to rushing toward the future and not staying present in the moment. Isn't it odd to think about how school systems do not consider having a course that discusses real-life predicaments that students will face? Why is that? No offense to those who enjoy or teach trigonometry, but that subject has yet to show any benefit in my life, so why was it emphasized so much to pass? Instead of having a passing grade requirement for trigonometry, they should've had the same for economic and personal finance. Imagine the type of financial knowledge you would have if that was something you were being taught in high school for four years instead of one or in college. Go more in-depth about financial literacy and make it mandatory for all undergraduate students to complete two years of the course(s). Classes on emotional intelligence, handling intimate and platonic relationships, and being prepared for the real world would have sufficed more than other courses that were requirements in high school and college. In this technological world we are in, a lot of the things we lack information on we research and gain knowledge through the internet, which can be a good or bad thing. Some could argue that the lack of this information is the parent(s) or guardian(s) fault; however, what if they are not fully knowledgeable on the information themselves? It's impossible to teach something that has not been taught to you personally. Patience seems like a trait that only a select few may have, but when you think about it, we are all patient to high levels, but that trait may be only focused on specific things within your life. How can you improve on implementing patience in most facets of your life? From experience, I had to realize not to get too emotional about things that did not work in my favor. It is easier said than done because there are times when all you can do is wonder and ask why. Why? No, seriously, I want to know why? Once I got over that immature phase, my perspective of things began to change because I felt I was being instructed to analyze my life at that current moment.

Am I lacking something I should have, and is this moment helping me develop or redefine an existing trait? Most of the time, this happens to be the answer to your issues. Take an internal inventory of areas that need improvement, but do not forget to list the positive traits you have as well.

On Sight

Yes it was your smile,
Your style,
The way you sang all through the night
Meeting someone for the first time and knowing
That's your Soulmate is an interesting sight
You honestly saved me
Theoretically from this compelling world
Becoming distance from shallowing hearts,
I'm thankful to find true love
I knew it was meant to be when
Unintentionally you played a song that was special to me
How could you unlock this treasure chest of emotions inside of me?
Tapping my face to see if I'll wake out of REM
You let out a calming chuckle
As if you understand
How ecstatic I am to be in your presence
No time apart is something that seems destined
The eye of my storm when I become a bit rattled
My flower that's presented from the depths of the gravel
Taking my hand in matrimony was our first step to infinite love
Pray our memory never fade so we can remember how everything was
At last
This bachelor lifestyle is coming to an end
Happy to say I'm hanging the jersey up
And throwing my cards all in
Glad to know you choose to be with me in this wild society
That's filled with broken promises
And high levels of anxiety
Because they're worried about the karma
They're going to get
So they continue playing dirty
Until everyone they come across needs to be rinsed
Thank you for being amazing
In many different ways
If I was to list out why
I wouldn't stop writing till twenty-88
I'll drop everything to be on the way
Shoutout to God
For allowing us to make our bond

Stronger everyday
I know I'm the prize
But you're like the Medal of Honor
So rare and mystique
I had to get down on one knee
Because you're one of kind
This I see within your eyes
The guardians of your soul
That deserves a dozen roses
whenever you may cry
A dozen orchids for your uniqueness that resides
And a single Lotus that symbolizes God's grace
For connecting us & presenting a pleasant future
For us to embrace
The two things I fear is God
And being separated from you
Couldn't imagine continuing life w/o my Queen,
My Baby,
My Sun,
My Moon,
The one I revolve around
And who knows my truths
The one that adores me for me
And not just what I bring
This admiration is so strong
That it feels I'm living in a dream
Even when I sleep
This fantasy becomes more than what it seems
You'll forever be mine and I'll forever be yours
Let's leave a blueprint
So everyone can learn how to build and walk through this door.

Point of Emphasis for On Sight:

This poem was inspired by an older lady I met one day in Florida. She probably would not recall our conversation, but it's unbelievable how much of an impact you could have in someone's life just by a simple conversation. I was her Uber driver, and we started the conversation as simply as anyone could, "Where are you from originally and what do you do for work?". We get into her explaining how she met her husband and believing in love at first sight. Before this conversation, I did not believe in the notion of "love at first sight" because how could you gain so much love for someone you do not know from Ying to Yang? Meaning you do not know the good and bad things about this particular person, so it is impossible to love them; maybe a strong admiration but not love. Well, I would be the first to say I was utterly wrong with that mindset because after she went into depth about their first date, it was clear that this was her soulmate. That is a day I truly look forward to seeing because there are so many fraudulent people in this world that it's ridiculous. Society shames people that show love, whether it's in a relationship or platonic, but it is fantastic to see we are making a change of giving someone their flowers or showing our admiration for them. Nothing is remarkable about being heartless. It only brings depressing emotions because you feel you cannot trust anyone and think you must do things alone. I had a stint when I was heartless because I wanted to impress friends and ensure I was not being played out here, but it led me nowhere. It's wild that the older you get, you realize how the more you pour into so many people, the more you could feel drained on the backend. You become burnt out, which could lead to many things transpiring. That is why finding that one person for you is one of the most incredible things that could ever happen in life. Of course, they're going to get on your nerves, and there may be someone that seems to be a better fit for you on the outside. However, for anyone reading this, THE GRASS IS NOT ALWAYS GREENER ON THE OTHER SIDE. I am not saying stay in the dead-end situation-ship, relationship, or marriages but consider everything your significant other brings to the table and then make your final decision. When you submit to this final decision, you cannot tether with the additional option in mind because that is how you play yourself. Seen too many people get out of a relationship because they want to be a bachelor, a.k.a "Be Outside," and it literally brought no asset to their lives. Please make the intelligent decision, do not settle for mediocracy, and stop comparing your love life to the fake happy couples on Instagram.

Excuse-Moi (Excuse Me)

Excuse me miss
I'm sorry to stop you along your way
But I had to introduce myself
To a woman that gives off an aura
Nothing short of marvelous
I know the dead-end compliments
You receive are becoming obnoxious
Nowadays,
You cannot decipher the fraudulent from the honest
Because everyone's first impression is of a person
They portray to be
But my intentions are to invest into you properly
Starting with a solid foundation
Like getting to know your name
Have to make sure I have the spelling right
For the dinner reservation that's being set
In the upcoming days
You're so used to being independent
So this type of catering is new
But enough about that,
I'm intrigued to learn more about you
What are the things that make you
Smile and cry so I know
What and what not to do
What are your plans?
What are some things you enjoy
That nobody ever knew?
I'm not asking just to waste time
Like I said, an investment is on my mind
But I get it
You'll believe that in due time
I respect it though
Because that shows you do not
Entertain any and everything out here,
Your standards are higher
And I'm happy to know
I made it into an exclusive tier
Not that I'm surprised,
We both symbolize excellence

Imagine what could be obtain with each other equally invested
Beyond a beautiful sight
I know at this point I have proven my worthiness
Because you won't look away from my eyes
In yours, I see all of the times
You've gave people a chance and they took it for granted
As much as you wanted to give up on love
You knew eventually the right one was close in distance
They will come interested in your spirit and not only
Your physical appearance
They will bring profit into your life
And not turn into an expense
They will give you the affection you desire
Beyond the realms in which we exist
Protect you from all of the harm in sight
And continuing to keep that promise
Even after separating from this life
Deep down you're ready to be loved
And let those indestructible walls go
I feel equally the same
And I'm not ashamed to say so
I understand real love takes perseverance
With patience along the way
As long as we have an agreement to see it through
I'm content with all the good and bad that'll come our way

<u>Point of Emphasis for Excuse-Moi (Excuse Me):</u>

Inspired by a favorite song of mine by one of my favorite artists, Excuse Me Miss by Jay Z was a song I played right before creating this poem. (Sidenote: every time I read this poem; I have the urge to play that song. I hope that you receive the same urge as well.) Analyzing that song shows how the mindset of a man can change when he finds a woman he is interested in. To be transparent, I have been blessed to connect with some beautiful women. From the United Kingdom, Germany, Spain, the Midwest, the South, and to a place with an area code of 757, they come in abundance. However, out of all these women, you could come across some that will have an everlasting effect on your life. Another transparent moment, this has happened to me multiple times and to some of them, I should have taken the chance to see what could have been with our situations. Here's a question for those reading this in a relationship: what caught your attention about your significant other? Was it that they were so indifferent from the others that it sparked an interest in you? It's interesting how one person can look at someone and think they are average, while another can look at the same person and see a treasure. Regarding the context of this poem, I wanted to approach it to show how someone genuinely interested will approach you. We all have dealt with much nonsense in our lives, so pay attention to the signs of someone genuinely interested in you.

The Getaway

Silence……
Peace……
Stillness……
All of the things I look forward to gaining when I arrive
Temporary happiness is on the way in due time
My escape from this simulation used to come in different forms
The one that seems to be the worst for me
Is the one I adore
The adrenaline I receive in the moments of takeoff
Pushes all anxiety away while we're aloft
I can't even recall why I was anxious in the first place
Guess you can tell I'm close to arrival
When I'm here, I'm my most vulnerable
Saying things short of honorable
Trying to figure out where's the last piece
To the puzzle of this internal trial
The tribulations tried to break me down
But I emerged through the concrete
I'm starting to understand why they consider
Life such an intricate thing now
You notice this the more you grow
I take a seat once I begin to feel my emotions overflow
Where are all the things I was looking for
That I said would be here when I'm here
Thoughts that linger as I take a sip of this potion
Why do most of my plans seem to get ruined?
The puff and past are now in motion
The sky begins to cry as it absorbs my pain
It sees me indulge into these negative things
It sees the unwanted thoughts creeping into my brain
This is not anything similar to how the first time became
Guess the body's becoming immune
This was supposed to be my escape
Now my Zen is ruined
I've tried other methods
But nothing gets me through it
I've indulged into other things
But this place brings more pleasure than pain
Escaping the reality for a small portion of time

___

I know it's wrong but please just try to understand one's mind
You don't know what you'll do until you're put in that position
We love to say what we wouldn't do
And suggest things that person should be doing
But just for a moment
Try to grasp the perspective that individual
Is projecting in real time
We're all hurt adults that deal with pain
Some just keep it confined

Point of Emphasis for The Getaway:

Judgment is what is wrong with the world. It's not a generational thing; it's a human species thing. Something looks foreign to a person, and they instantly want to judge like their way is always the right way. A lot of these beliefs and understandings come from past down stories that were manipulated, but nobody ever wants to speak on that. In complete honesty, I can say that I was an individual that would judge why certain people would do drugs and commit certain crimes, but life showed me that you never know what you would do or think until you were put in that position. It's so much judgment still happening in the world, but it's nice to see that it has a positive trajectory. However, regarding the topic above, what should a person do to help them get out of the situation when they have tried every positive method? I do not know the answer and wish someone could explain it because some people try other methods but fall victim to alcohol and drug abuse. Another transparency moment, I did not understand the negative powers alcohol could portray. I never will forget the day I found out a close friend of mine passed away while I was living overseas. One of the things that hurt me the most in this situation was when I saw people talk about it on social media when nothing was confirmed yet, I was about to message him to let him know I was just checking on him to make sure he was good, but I never went to send the message because I didn't think they were talking about him. It was not until I received a call from my close friend that confirmed everything. Instantly I went numb. The pain I felt was something I hadn't felt in a while since both of my grandmothers passed away. I did not know what to do but cry my sorrows away until I passed out from being drunk. Even as the days went by, looking at photos, or thinking about all the hilarious moments we had as brothers, brought more and more pain. Even being unable to attend the funeral or even confine with his family hurts me to this day. At that moment, though, I wouldn't realize that I would feel that moment three more times in that year; it got to the point I was scared to answer the phone because all of my terrible news either came from a phone call or text. I never told anyone this, but that was the year drinking became a little bit heavier in my life, but that was also the time I realized that my coping mechanism was taking words from my brain and bringing them to life to paint a picture that even someone that is the opposite of me could understand, the true meaning of the gift and the curse. The only thing I could say about this situation is that it is more to the spectrum than what the normal eye can see. Most of the time, unsolved trauma is the reason, but consider that the next time you are quick to judge someone.

A Dedication

Worst nightmare

The worst nightmares are the ones you remember over and over
again
I received my prayer
But not in a form I wished
I finally got my chance to speak to you again
To give you updates on my life
But I was so at peace
The important topics didn't even cross my mind
It was just like a normal day
How it used to be
Jumping topic to topic so naturally
I wish I could remember all of the things you said
I still see your face, but your voice is omitted
When I awoke I had to remember you are not in the physical
realm
And that is what hurt my soul
Because it felt like I lost you again
I never judge when someone drinks or do drugs to cope with
the pain
Sometimes that spiritual connection is the only thing that keeps
us sane
Sane in an insane world
How does that even work
I'm more in peace when I sleep
Entering inside your world

For My Brothers

I shake my head in disbelief every time I hear your names
Damn,
My heart goes for the ones dealing with similar pain
It's been some years and truthfully I thought I'll be out of my
grievance stage
But the daily task that I do
Always reminds me of all of you
From the songs to certain sayings, to on the basketball courts
playing
It hurts
It truly does
I can't hold up this lie
Reasons why I cherish memories in these moments of time
Can never question The Almighty
As it says within the scriptures
I'm just thankful I was able to be a part of your motion picture

Point of Emphasis for A Dedication:

*This poem was written in two different parts, with the first half being about
family members that have transitioned into the next life and the second
being about friends who have done the same. At times a person's demise
can be arduous to register in my brain. The fact that a person could be
breathing, thinking, and reacting to things and then not be here forever
physically is a feeling that can never become easy to deal with. I realized
that writing helps in those days when I am grieving. This point of emphasis
will be relatively short because many of the emotions I have to say are
already within the poem above. The last thing I would say to the reader is
that grief does not have a time limit, embrace the emotions you are feeling
and continue to be level-headed to get through this specific phase.*

All on You

These organizations are implemented to say they care
But cold heartedly don't
They want to see you fall
And engage with
Non-prescribed drugs,
Alcohol and nicotine,
Numbing you to what's going on
Nobody cares
About your bills being past due
Charging crazy interest
When life is throwing haymakers at you
Nobody cares
When your stomach is arguing with you
Drinking water
Envisioning it's a dish from a
3-course menu
Nobody cares when you're in a jam
From a failed plan
They only care to say, "I told you so",
When you didn't take heed
To what they said
Nobody cares when your love life
Fails in a multitude of ways
Life telling you to settle
For someone you'll later
Consider as just a roommate
Now that you see the truth
What are you going to do?
Cry? Complain?
Only pray for things to change,
Like faith without work isn't dead
According to what the Good Book say
Nothing is going to happen
Until you make something happen
Expecting success without work
Is like waiting on a non-delivered package
Don't be comfortable with a life of complacency
We fall down but we get up
So continue striving for excellency

Point of Emphasis for All on You:

In full transparency, year 26 is running its course on me. I've always been a glass-half-full individual, but I'll be lying if I said it was easy to keep that mindset even with everything I was dealing with. The title for the poem was first going to be named, "Nobody Cares," with the expression of saying you cannot get the help you want unless you help yourself. An extreme case, but it's like seeing homeless people on the street. You want to help as much as possible, but your help can only go so far if it's not reciprocated on the opposite end. Even though the poem was written with the inspiration of giving motivation, this point of emphasis must express the real talks that an individual has with themselves and not necessarily with other people. In my situation, I was too prideful. I did not want to receive any help but wanted to help my entire community and some. Wise words from my fraternal brother Joshua Boone, "You can give out blessings, but you must learn how to receive them as well. If you don't, it messes up the flow of life". That is one of the most realistic phrases I've ever heard. I am a natural giver that doesn't accept people helping me out very well. I've gained many things from putting my feet on the ground and getting to work. I understand the struggle, so I want to be able to help those around me. As a man, I feel that helping others find and develop their path is one of my primary purposes (See how my pride thinks). However, going through hardships showed how stupid this mindset was to have. I always heard how it takes a village to get to the top of the mountain, but I always felt that didn't apply to me (An Aquarius Mindset lol). We receive lessons from God to help us understand certain things about ourselves when pressure is applied. Are you an excuse-maker? Do you not do well with constructive criticism? Do you have a "woe is me" mindset? These are all the things that slow down the progression of your greatness. The first step of positive progression is becoming aware of your negative flaws because ignorance is not bliss in this situation. Next is being patient with yourself enough to understand that you will have days when you are on the right path and other days when you are slipping; that is okay. Rome was not built overnight, the Pyramids of Giza were not created in a week, and Dubai was not developed as a luxury city in a month. Excellence takes time and no book, therapist, friend, family, or significant other can tell you when your time is nigh. Stay patient and enjoy your progression.

Jollity

Addicted to happiness
&
Addicted to genuine love
Two things working together
To keep me staying above
All this nonsense shown on a daily,
I'm just glad to know my soul
Is always feeling elated
Elated to being in the presence
Of family and friends
I cherish these moments
Wishing I could live them again
This is what life is all about
Being a part of moments
That our brains can never doubt
Showing and spreading love
Things I cannot go without
It's an amazing feeling I wish
Everyone was comfortable getting
I pray to keep it flowing
While I continue to keep on giving it

Point of Emphasis for Jollity

Jollity means being cheerful; what are things that make you cheerful? Why do they make you cheerful? It's incredible to know that you have these things that bring you joy because surprisingly, there are people in the world who do not and are feigning to have a small sample of pleasure you are having. I am big on taking photos and videos because I love reminiscing. I gained that trait from my grandmother and great-grandmother because they were quick to throw a picture in the photo album. But as I get older, I understand the significance behind that because think about how we can stop a moment in time and keep it replaying in our mental catalog or being able to record a moment and relive it repeatedly. Those are things people take for granted in life. I always said that I hope that when we transition into the next life, God will allow us to relive joyful moments. Too many I would love to relive, but I also know I have an infinite amount to make in the future.

<u>As a Man</u>

As a man
It is my obligation to protect you from harm's way
My obligation to make sure you're going about life
The right way
As a man
I know the things you say you adore,
Thinking I'm not listening
Until you see the items are placed at your door
As a man
You must understand I need to do my own thing
Not in a way that'll disrespect you
But just understand
I have to play the game of life a certain way
I'll always be attentive to
What is going on
And trust my absence will later pay off
Any expense you have in your brain
It's so fortunate
It can even pay off the tangibles
Ten times
You think I want to lose a women
That defines the true meaning of divine
As a man
Understand I'm learning to take your word
For as it is
I've been involved with plenty women
That had a significant other living in their crib
They see what you have
So I can't be mad at the attempt
But remember with you I'm more than content
Because you bring that equalized peace
That a man will forever need
Never forget your worth
And how much you mean to me
As a man just know I will always have your back for life
No matter if you're wrong or right
As a man I'm hoping
You are understanding what a man needs
And since you do, I appreciate you for cherishing me

Point of Emphasis for As a Man:

If women wanted to understand what a man wants from them, these are a few things. After asking many of my friends in relationships, communication can go a long way. It's a simple two-way street if you play your position. I know the stigma of men nowadays, but we're not all like that. I must represent the solid ones out there and state, "We are not attracted to the buffoonery, the buffoonery is attracted to us". With great power comes great responsibility and with a good man comes things trying to knock him off the path of excellency. Truthfully, this poem could go both ways because it is women out here who are not with the buffoonery and handling business as well. Social media only idolize shallow individuals, so at times, it can seem like its only fake women left (aka birds), but honestly, they still exist but are secluded. One thing I wish is for my generation and an older generation to swap places for a week so they can understand the things we have to deal with daily when it comes to getting to know someone or even dating them. Do you think they would be able to withstand it? It's a harsh feeling to deal with when you direct message someone just to be left on read and sent in their group chat (I'm not saying this happened to me, hopefully not). Furthermore, as a man was written to at least help women understand we are wired differently and at times, we show our love differently. It doesn't mean we don't want or love you; some have an interesting way of showing it. Trust in those moments of distress; you will realize who will have your back and who will not.

As a Woman

The things you go through I could never understand
Your essence is life, every other species
Should bow down to your command
Your powers are dangerous that's why you're ridiculed the most
And I notice the nonsense that's why I shielded you from being riposte
No need to succumb to their levels, stay focused and stay grounded
Make sure to take inventory on the ones that's surrounding
As a Woman
I noticed that word is merely an acronym
To symbolize the traits you have within
First being well-round which you need to succeed
It's more than book smarts
That's placing you in front of your dreams
Next is observant which unfortunately
Stays for multiple days, I see it as annoyance, but you see it as
Protecting my ways because you know no one can hold it down
For me the way you do
Internally I'm grateful even if that's not
What I'm physically showing you
Next is magnificent which is self-explanatory
Just glace in the mirror to see the beauty of your story
Next is enticing which may be my favorite of them all
So alluring that you can get any and everything you want
Lastly is nourishing because you're essential to existence itself
A world without you is an everlasting hell
As a Woman
I know you see yourself as a light
That's always dim but you need to know
Your light is as bright as 100,000 Lumen
Look it up so you'll get the analogy
As a Woman
You love to be taught things
So now I'm viewed as enticing
But you're the one that's attractive
That's why it's hard to understand
That you don't see yourself as beautiful
Every time that you can,
I know some have off days, but I don't see that with you
You are perfection and never think that this is untrue

As a Woman
I'm glad that I'm your opposite
So I can be engulfed with your treasures
Continue to be life's professor, so I can receive all your lessons

Point of Emphasis for As a Woman:

Tupac Shakur created Keep Your Head Up: this is my version of women's empowerment. After reading As a Man and As a Woman, it is fair enough to say no gender can understand the other. So why do we continue to try? I'm guilty of this sometimes and trying to understand was such a headache that I had to stop. So many conversations with women that explained what they thought of themselves on a day-to-day basis. The most confusing thing is a beautiful woman feeling she is ugly. It's unfathomable to me because I want to ask, do you look at yourself in the mirror? I know of a woman I encountered for a short time that was stunning but didn't see herself in the same perspective at times. I used to see her pictures and be confused because in every angle she looked amazing; with glasses on or off, she looked terrific, and even when she was casual, she looked better than some women in their Sunday best. Seeing how the eyes can play many tricks on us is unbelievable. This is the most challenging point of emphasis to speak on because most of the things I wanted to say are above in the poem. It is like the mic being dropped; what more can I say? No matter how annoying women become in my life, I could never discard them because I need them more than they'll ever know. Women raised me, which may be why my appreciation goes beyond the parameters. I know you will have those days when you do not feel like it but continue shining bright; you never know who you are inspiring.

Forgiveness

I wrote this poem for those in need
For those in distress
For those who won't let their inner child be at rest
At your current age you feel you have everything under control
But the key to life is understanding that's not how everything goes
You've made some great decisions
And some you may regret
But never feel like you're the only soul dealing with this
See we all have things we've said we let go
But never did
Things we tell ourselves we'd forgot
But gets replayed in our head
With its own automation
& then,
We mask all the emotional attachment that comes with it
Feeling like this negative cycle will never end
But at the end of day
You must forgive yourself once again
No family or friend can amend
What's going on within
Forgive yourself of all transgressions
& travel along the road of peace
my good friend
Forgive yourself of all transgressions
& travel along the road of peace
my good friend

Point of Emphasis for Forgiveness:

I _place this as the book's last poem because I want it to resonate with the reader. I used to think that if I wanted to stop thinking about something, all I had to do was forget it; that idea failed me over a hundred times. Another method I thought worked would be writing it in a journal to get the thoughts out of my head which failed me a thousand more times. The last result was telling myself that it did not affect me and that I was just being too sensitive; I lost count of how many times I tried to do that. Forgiveness is a life practice that only becomes better over time. No need to put so much pressure on your life because you are unique at the end of the day. You are breathing air right now, and you can change your life at any point in time. The last transparent moment I will have in the book will explain a part of my life's journey. I hope whoever reads this part will understand that it does not matter what your life was before; you can change what you want. Prior to starting my life journey at Old Dominion University, my young teen and adolescent times were interesting. My life did a complete 180 from how I was in middle and high school. It was not because I wanted to put on a persona that was not me like some people I knew, but because I made the vow to be comfortable with myself (And if they did not like me, f*ck them). This brought many people I could connect with on multiple levels, which only increased the higher I elevated in college. However, there is one moment I can say forever changed my life and made me realize my inner powers. It was around my junior year, and I was heavily interested in joining this fraternity named Alpha Phi Alpha Inc. I wanted to ensure I was a great candidate, so I focused on my academics, volunteered more, and ensured I was active in the community. I did not know anything about fraternities, so daily I wondered if I was going about getting noticed the right way. A time came when I found out they were not interested in me as a candidate. It hurt a little bit, but I was determined to do what I needed to do to join. Unfortunately, my grandmother transitioned before I could tell her I wanted to become an Alpha during this time. That added to the hurt but even motivated me to keep going. Months go by, and I receive an email stating how my hard work is being recognized during a banquet my school is hosting. It portrayed the idea of being important, so I was about to tell my friends and family to join me. However, something in my soul kept telling me to attend this event first to ensure everything was accurate before I invited them. I get to the event and find my name on the table, so I start to get excited. I flip through the handbook on the table and go to the section for the category I was being honored in, and my name is not in sight. I instantly thought I was just in the wrong section, so I continued flipping through the book, and still my name was nowhere in sight._

I went back and looked at the email to ensure I was invited, and as I already knew, it stated that I was indeed invited to this event. It even states how I must RSVP to let them know I am attending. Still in delusion, I continued to wait to see if they would call my name eventually. I did not know how much staying for the event would hurt me because if I had known that MY ENTIRE TABLE WOULD GET UP TO RECEIVE AN AWARD, I WOULD HAVE LEFT IMMEDIATELY. IT WAS ABOUT 13 PEOPLE SITTING AT THAT TABLE, AND 12 OUT OF THE 13 HAD AN AWARD TO TAKE HOME. I cannot lie, I drove straight home angrily, sat in the parking lot, and cried (I mean one of those deep sorrow cries). I cried because I was so furious. Why do I continue to get the short end of the stick with everything I want to do? Why am I such a failure? All these things are going through my mind to the point that I was just about to say forget being in college because I am a failure and will not do anything in life; why should I continue to get a degree? But at that moment, it was an instant change in my life that even to this day I do not know what type of inner force was ignited. I made a silent vow to myself that I would never be a failure ever in my life again. I promised myself that it did not matter what happened the years before because the following year would be different for me. 2018 was tough, and not many people understood what my family and I were even dealing with. Having my mother say we had to move from our home to my grandmother's house during winter break, losing my grandmother while in her home (the same place I lived for a portion of time), hearing her in pain, seeing how she was the morning before I left to go to work at Walmart, getting off of work and finding out she passed right before Christmas Eve, having to see my mother struggle to find a new place to live, having people in her life do her wrong in a multitude of ways, trying to figure out how to be a grown man at 21 when I did not have a positive image of it in my household, trying to obtain things I wanted in my life at the time, having to stop communicating with a girl I admired strongly, and other things I cannot disclose. I had a breaking point. I had a "f*ck it" mindset when doing what I needed to do to succeed. The year after I made that promise to myself, everything I said would happen came to fruition. The catalyst to overcoming that phase was forgiving myself for everything I felt I did not accomplish in life. I felt like a failure since I was a teenager and never had the strength to tell myself that everything is okay. Once I did that, it was like the sky's limitation became infinite, and I *started to accomplish more than I ever thought I would. In conclusion, I know it sounds repetitive, but please learn how to forgive yourself. Do not succumb to past images of who you used to be because today is a new day, next week is a new week, and next year is a new year.*

Thank you for getting to this point of the book. I hope you enjoyed it, and more are to come in the foreseeable future.

Sincerely,
Mr. Talik Jordan

Made in the USA
Middletown, DE
05 October 2023

40326544R00033